CW01638851

CAMEL
TROPHY

CAMEL TROPHY 1994

CHRIS BENNETT

Photographs and text by
Chris Bennett

Edited by
Richard Thomas

Page design by
Cathie Howell

Produced by
Golden Gate Productions
for the publishers
LRO Mail Order Ltd
Anglian House
Botesdale
Diss, Norfolk IP22 1DT

ISBN 1 873564 06 6

Typesetting, colour origination
and printing by
Micropress Printers Ltd
27 Norwich Road
Halesworth
Suffolk IP19 8BX

Additional material on the
1994 Camel Trophy
appeared in Land Rover
Owner International magazine.
Back copies are available from
the publishers at the address
above.

© Chris Bennett

All rights reserved. No part of
this book may be reproduced
in any form without the
written permission of the
publishers

About the author

Chris Bennett has been photographing Land Rovers since 1991 when he produced a colour picture book dedicated to the subject. Since then the bug has bitten and the involvement increased, much of his material finding a home in *Land Rover Owner International magazine*. The opportunity to participate in Camel Trophy was one eagerly anticipated; for the action orientated photographer it's a perfect subject.

***Camel Trophy 1994 - Argentina Paraguay Chile* is the sixth book bearing Chris Bennett's name. Most recently he produced a book dedicated to the Benetton Formula One motor racing team, another on the Lamborghini Countach supercar and two further volumes featuring state of the art jet-fighter aircraft.**

Photo: Nick Dimbleby

Acknowledgements

It would be impossible to name everyone here who helped, directly or indirectly, in the production of this book. For the many people I met on Camel Trophy - participants, organisers and journalists - a collective 'cheers' will have to suffice. However, I would like to express my sincere thanks to Iain Chapman, Duncan Barbour and Nick Horne of Global Event Management; Robert Chandler of Worldwide Brands; Debbie Watts of West End PR; Tony Jardine and Nigel 'Q' Quilter of Jardine PR; Bob and Joe Ives; Lee Farrant; Dave Stevens of Cotswold Camping and let's not forget Damien Taft, Mark Cullum and Paul 'Chad' Chadderton who patiently endured my presence in the Team UK Discovery for 14 days and 3,051 kilometres. Lastly, a very special thank you to my good friend Richard Thomas who ultimately made this unique opportunity possible.

If I walk away with one lasting memory it will be of the small towns and villages that we visited, of the wide-eyed wonderment and delight in those young faces and of experiencing the warm open welcome of these people, people who may be poor in material wealth but are rich in honesty and kindness. Camel Trophy touched and enriched their lives and the lives of the many international participants from around the world. Long may it continue to do so. CB

Nikon

All images reproduced within this volume were shot exclusively with Nikon F4 cameras fitted with Nikkor lenses and loaded with Fuji Velvia RVP and RDP film stocks. Nikon cameras have accompanied the author on his exploits around the world, time and again proving their worth and reliability where it counts - in the heat of the action - be that the steamy jungles of Malaysia or at 30,000 ft over Iceland in an F-15 fighter. To date, Camel Trophy is probably the ultimate test in adverse conditions. Nikon came through with flying colours.

THE CAMEL TROPHY began in 1980 when three West German teams spent twelve days driving 1600 kms along the Transamazonica highway through the mud and heat of the Amazon jungle. Over the years, the event has grown in size and complexity, with 1994 seeing eighteen national teams competing for the Trophy.

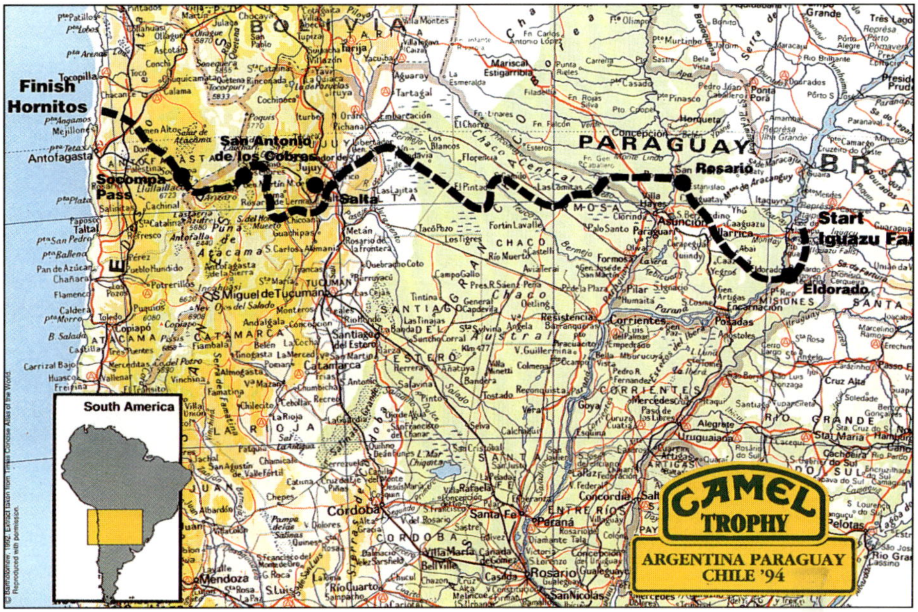

Using only Land Rover-built vehicles, the teams and support crews penetrate deep into often hostile and almost always beautiful landscapes. With a special concern for the environment, the convoy uses only existing roads and tracks.

The competition for the Camel Trophy itself takes place through a series of special tasks which combine tests of driving skills and navigation with individual mental and physical tasks. These tasks are held on specially designated sites while team members work together on the convoy sections to help one another through.

For me, the opportunity to participate in the 1994 Camel Trophy expedition to Argentina, Paraguay and Chile, was one that I had longed for, but seldom believed would become a reality. Only two 'participating journalists' from each competing nation can actually take part in the entire event, travelling in the convoy in their national vehicle, effectively becoming an integral part of the team. I was thrilled to be invited to join the British Team of Mark Cullum and Damien Taft in their Discovery to represent *Land Rover Owner International* magazine.

Camel Trophy '94 was to prove rather different from others in the event's 15 year history. We were to pass through three South American countries, each of which would present very varied conditions and, therefore, photographic opportunities. In particular, our passage through the Andes was an experience I shall never forget; it's just a pity that the true dramatic beauty of this region can never be fully reproduced on two dimensional celluloid.

Within this book I have tried, both in pictures and words, to introduce Camel Trophy in a rather different and unique manner. Hopefully, for those enthusiasts not quite so fortunate or privileged as myself, the volume will offer a realistic, personal reflection and insight into this legend in adventure - Camel Trophy, Class of '94.

Now that my Camel Trophy is well and truly over, I can look back on it with very fond memories, especially of the wonderful camaraderie that prevailed and of new found friends and kindred spirits. It really has been an experience of a lifetime and one that I feel proud to have both successfully achieved and to have been associated with.

CHRIS BENNETT

An orderly parade of immaculate, factory fresh Land Rover Discoverys and Defender 110s await the start of Camel Trophy '94. One thing is for sure, at the end of their three week trial of endurance these vehicles won't be quite so pristine. The competitors' Discoverys are at present some 150 kms down river at Estancia Eldorado, these examples being marshal and support vehicles.

12:00 midday on Saturday 16th April Day 1. Following the lavish and colourful flag-off ceremony at Hotel Internacional, Mark Cullum and Damien Taft, alias Team United Kingdom, run down to the base of Iguazu Falls on the Iguazu River. This is the start of Camel Trophy '94 and our 2,500 kms journey of adventure.

Earlier that morning our intrepid duo took time out to study the rules and regulations of their forthcoming Special Tasks, in this case Task D – a vehicle recovery scenario set in an old quarry. The Special Tasks which are completed in two sections at the start and finish of the Trophy expedition, can be both complicated and confusing, often involving a number of teams working together. They are run rigidly to the letter of the rules and therefore it's wise to study and understand these thoroughly.

Down by the riverside Olli Kangas the male contingent of Team Scandinavia, receives the attentions of his female partner in the form of 27 year old Christel Persson, a lawyer from Malmö in Sweden. Camel Trophy '94, the fifteenth in this prestigious, male-dominated event's history, was the first in which women were actually to participate as team members. In addition to Christel, 50% of the French team was to be female in the person of Carine Duret.

Johnson
175

It's all aboard and full steam ahead for a four hour high speed inflatable boat ride, navigating both the Iguazu and Parana rivers, and in doing so, breeching the frontiers of Brazil, Argentina and Paraguay. Contained within this rapid, bouncing armada are the 36 international competitors, that's two from each of the eighteen participating nations, plus a similar number of us 'participating journalists'. Beneath a blisteringly hot sun this method of transport is ideal, but I'm very glad of my water bottle – never been so thirsty.

Suitably kitted out in response to the inclement conditions Mark provides partner Damien with precise instructions on one of the log obstacle tasks. Saturated by rain, the logs had transformed into greasy tightropes; difficult at the best of times, this task was now virtually impossible. A total of nine Special Tasks including physical trials such as orienteering and bridge building, together with driving involving Terratrip and obstacle negotiation were to be completed in this first set.

Left: Here at Eldorado, on our second day the blue sky and sunshine was displaced by torrential, steamy rain. Although making the completion of tasks much more difficult, the rain was unsuccessful in diminishing the spirit of competitors or marshals.

Above: Olli provides the directions as companion Christel, at the wheel of the Scandinavian Discovery, prepares to challenge her skills against another log obstacle. Her task was made rather easier in that it was completed prior to the heavens opening. Nicknamed 'Jurassic Park' this ingenious log construction was the brainchild of Duncan Barbour and featured an elongated 'pyramid' followed by a reversal 'v' gulley. This task also issued many vehicles with their first battle scars, the driver's door sills and front wheel rims proving most vulnerable.

CAMEL
Mark Cullum

Etienne van Eeden proudly displays the sole remaining evidence of his pair of jungle boots. He, together with fellow members of Team South Africa apparently left their boots rather close to the camp fire overnight! This is the first time that South Africa has entered Camel Trophy but there certainly was no lack of interest. Etienne, a jet-fighter pilot, together with partner Klaus Hass were selected from nearly 70,000 applicants.

Monday 18th April Day 3.
Our final morning of tasks and the weather has improved dramatically — but not alas the fortunes of Team UK. On a rock-strewn natural obstacle task we suffer a badly worn tyre, probably the result of under inflation and over zealous driving. At the completion of this first set of tasks Switzerland are leading with the United Kingdom in 6th position. The special tasks are designed to challenge and evaluate physical endurance, mental agility, navigational and driving skills, in a 'controlled' situation.

Spirits are high. The tasks, for the time being at least, are behind us and ahead the 2,500 kms drive across South America. Excited – you bet. At 14:35 the 33 strong convoy is issued with national flags and prepares to drive down main street Eldorado, much to the obvious delight and appreciation of the enthusiastic local populace.

The Parana River separates Argentina from Paraguay and our way across is by ferry. Mark Cullum indulges in some international entente cordiale with a pair of Paraguayan naval officers.

CAMEL 8
CAMEL
TROPHY
LAND ROVER

One soon learns to take advantage of any and all washing opportunities en-route including, in this case the Parana River, as demonstrated by competitor Cullum.

The French team's mascot, don't worry though, Polly Parrot's only made of foam

The 33 strong convoy consists of 18 national team Discoverys plus the balance in support Discoverys and 110s. It requires two trips of the massive steel ferry to navigate this lot across the Parana and the sun is starting to descend as the first contingent takes to the water. Once safely on the other side and in Paraguay we take to mud tracks, driving for over six hours in the darkness, until finally pitching camp at 00:30.

Tuesday 19th April Day 4.
Up bounding with energy at 05:30 after only three and a half hours sleep. Strange thing is I feel remarkably fit considering lack of shut-eye over the past few days. Following a snack breakfast we're on the road again by 06:30, the intention being to get as many kilometres behind us today as possible. The tracks here are constructed rather more with four-hoofed than four-wheeled forms of motive power in mind. This vehicle seems to represent the family transport, complete with three generations aboad.

Travel for mile after mile on these dirt tracks of red mud. Although slippery in places, because there has been far less rain than expected, the going is not as tough as had been feared. The French duo of Carine Duret and Jean Yves Paillier let fly their Discovery, their multi-coloured mascot threatening to break free.

The convoy halts temporarily to regroup, permitting backmarkers to catch up. A perfect opportunity for a bite to eat and some international socialising.

DEFENDER
DISCOVERY
DEFENDER
L426 VAC

Still we are fortunate that rain has kept away. If these tracks had been wet they'd be both slippery and treacherous, but as it is we manage to maintain good time. Word reaches us though that further ahead trouble awaits.

We pass through the occasional small village of wooden shacks. The locals, who are obviously very poor, wave enthusiastically at us shouting 'ola' in greeting, especially the groups of kids. School's out for Camel Trophy! After all, this is probably the most dramatic event to have occurred in their young lives.

As the tracks gradually become drier so too the surface becomes more and more powdery. The convoy now starts to kick up plumes of dust in its wake, although as time would demonstrate, this was nothing to what awaited us later in the desert. Nevertheless it's an opportune moment for Junichi 'Waka' Wakabayashi from Kanagawa in Japan to break out his protective face mask.

Today we reach the town of Rosario in readiness for our second crossing, courtesy of the Paraguayan Navy. We had planned to cross the Paraguay River tonight but this idea was scuppered when the ferry was unavailable. However our stop at Rosario provided an opportunity to barter for supplies — biscuits, bottled water and even tins of local beer.

Left: Christel demonstrates to Carine, her French counterpart just how, in the face of treacherous odds, she managed to bring the Scandinavian vehicle through unscathed.

By 19:30 we arrive at our campsite, nice and early just for a change due to the enforced stop. Damien and Mark perform some minor repairs to their winch cable, it having been damaged during the tasks at Eldorado. This is the first suitable opportunity to conduct such repairs.

CAMEL
TROPHY
DEFENDER
DISCOVERY
LAND ROVER

Wednesday 20th April Day 5.
This morning we board the ferry to make the hour long crossing of the Paraguay River. Once again it requires two journeys to transport all the vehicles across and, fortunately for us, we go second, thus permitting an opportunity to make use of some washing facilities at Puerto Rosario. First proper bodily cleanse for a few days and, after the dust of yesterday, perfectly timed.

This gaucho, one of the traditional South American cowboys, is happy to admire the spectacle as Camel Trophy '94 passes by.

Ahead of us lies some pretty testing terrain. The 'Chaco' is notoriously boggy, although once again it is rather drier than predicted. The surrounding scenery is flat and marshy with lush green vegetation and tall palm-like trees.

CAMEL
TROPHY
DISCOVERY

During our Camel Trophy expedition we were to see many examples of weird and wonderful wildlife, generally of the smaller insect variety. With the noise created by 33 Land Rovers most of the bigger examples had plenty of advance warning of our presence. There were many exotic, beautiful coloured butterflies, some up to six inches across.

In its natural bush environment (to where it was safely returned) this stick insect would display perfect camouflage.

Another common but less inviting example of South America's wildlife are the many species of rather large spiders that seemingly abound. This particularly nasty looking three inch critter had spread its web across two small trees some six feet apart. A reminder to look where you're walking!

DEFENDER
L 422
VAC

As day turns into night our tracks gradually become heavily waterlogged, requiring extensive use of right foot and winch cable. Cameleers add their weight and muscle, rocking the 110 to assist its Superwinch. The broken right head lamp and bent number plate had become the victims, only moments earlier, of a catapulting shackle.

The luckless pilot of this management Discovery found that too much speed through these bogs can, on occasion, end in tears. However the vehicle is quickly righted and, having suffered no damage whatsoever, continues merrily on its way.

Thursday 21st April Day 6. The mud we encountered last night continues in earnest. We're negotiating the appropriately named 'Road to Hell', a track consisting of deep, glutinous mud. Ahead of us lies a stretch of water bog fully 100 yards long and three feet deep.

It's every man (and woman) to the shovels in an attempt to clear the way through but, for the participants of Camel Trophy '94, this is what the event is all about.

After some 45 minutes of hard graft the first vehicles manage to blast headlong through the bath of waterlogged mud and slime. Mark succeeds in driving the UK vehicle through at the first attempt, using plenty of speed and inertia, with the Land Rover rocking and rolling, leaping and bounding in protest.

CAMEL
TROPHY
DISCOVERY

But the going is slow and laborious on the famed 'Road to Hell'. No sooner does each individual vehicle plough through one mud section than it is confronted by yet another. Teamwork is the order of the day and, as the Japanese snatch the Discovery of Carlos Martinez free, the Brits perform a similar service for one of the support vehicles.

CAMEL
TROPHY

It was at Iguazu Falls that we first met the team representing South Africa, a firm bond of friendship quickly developing. For the duration of Camel Trophy '94 we worked closely with them — a fine bunch of guys. Not intimidated by a little mud and slime Etienne van Eeden, a jet-fighter pilot in the South African Air Force, gets stuck in to help release the UK vehicle.

CAMEL
TROPHY
DISCOVERY

The Japanese vehicle's Superwinch groans in response to the load as Tadashi Iio, alias 'One Ten', operates the remote control, his attention alert to partner Waka's instructions.

A queue of vehicles patiently await their turn as Klaus Hass blasts the SA Discovery through. We'd go from wet to dry but the further down the track we got the more water logged it became.

CAMEL
TROPHY
DISCOVERY
CAMEL
TROPHY
DISCOVERY

It's 14:40 and the convoy comes to an unscheduled halt. Having successfully struggled through six of these long, deep mud baths news reaches us that, almost unbelievably, we're going back the way we came. Event director Iain Chapman and lead scout Marc Day have reconnoitred the area ahead in the support helicopter. Apparently the sight that greets them is kilometre after kilometre of totally submerged ground — our proposed route is waterborne and impassable. The word is to backtrack, detour and pick up better roads to make up lost time. That's Camel Trophy.

At the start of the day the UK and SA vehicles were near the head of the convoy. Consequently, in reverse order we now find ourselves at the back and it's fully ninety minutes before the convoy's snail pace progress finally permits us to move. A perfect opportunity to catch up on some shuteye . . .

. . . or to perform those domestic chores like washing and drying of clothes and boots.

It's also an ideal chance to snatch a meal. A long night lies ahead and we don't know when we'll eat again. That's one lesson quickly learnt on Camel Trophy — always make full use of any opportunities.

Evening rolls in bringing with it mosquitoes as we tackle another now familiar bog section. By 22.00 it's pitch dark as, at last, the final big mud channel lies ahead, illuminated by our headlamp beams. Seemingly it is impossible to drive through, most vehicles getting a third of the way before losing momentum and bogging down. From here it requires the combined length of six kinetic ropes to haul them through to the other end.

CAMEL TROPHY
ADVENTURE WEAR
LAND ROVER

After regrouping, the convoy moves off to mark up some high speed tarmac kilometres and it's 03:00 before we finally stop to make camp. Won't be much sleep tonight however — bed at 03:45 only to be up again by 06:30 for an 07:30 start.

Friday 22nd April Day 7
Although the tracks we drive today are somewhat more substantial, overnight torrential rain has produced localised flooding, once again successfully slowing our progress.

Logistics on Camel Trophy are immense, one of the prime consumables being 'motion-lotion'. Well we wouldn't get very far without it. Sometimes refueling is accomplished at specially pre-arranged dumps and at other times, as in this case, by utilising regular petrol stations. The owner of this example at Estancia Primavera must have thought all his Christmases had arrived at once.

Even Camel Trophy has to abide by the rules and it takes two hours for all our passengers to be cleared at the Paraguay/Argentina border.

Just slipping and sliding on Route 86. Even though Ruta 86 is a key road, the surface still consists of nothing more than thick greasy mud, its treachery compounded by frequent bucket sized potholes. Mark Cullum fights for control as the UK team's Discovery pirouettes from side to side on the slippery surface, the vehicle's rear wheels constantly threatening to overtake those at the front. With confidence mounting despite the hazardous conditions our road speed is up to 60-80kph, the incredibly strong Discovery taking in its stride an inhuman barrage as we hit the bumps and holes at component-shattering velocities.

Arrive at the small town of Laguna Yema low on fuel — in fact we're on vapour. As we drive into town the convoy is mobbed by hundreds of locals, kids, parents and grandparents, all eager for stickers and souvenirs. The kids are so polite and timid and one feels that they who are so poor and have so little are both good and honest.

Experiencing the brief but intense joy that Camel Trophy brings to these people's lives makes one proud to be part of it.

Carlos seems to have adopted a new pet, or should that be the other way around? Didn't realise that locusts are so damn big, it's little wonder that swarms of these creatures can cause so much devastation to crop harvests.

Dogan Akcora is celebrating his birthday and late in the wee hours we all repair to the Turkish vehicle for an impromptu party and sing-song. Olli Kangas from Team Scandinavia together with his guitar are welcome additions, as are the ever enthusiastic Japanese duo 'Waka' and 'One Ten'.

An oriental reflection perhaps on our enforced rapid pace of the past 48 hours.

Using narrow winding tracks we start to climb deep into the foothills of the Andes. To the sides are dramatic drops that can all too easily become very real, trapping the unwary or incautious. It's only the presence of a small tree that prevents this Discovery and its fortunate crew from rolling end over end, down into Rio Pasajeo.

Monday 25th April Day 10
The Andes offer some of the most spectacular views in the history of the Camel Trophy. At 10,000 feet the winding track that we have just ascended lends depth to this breathtaking vista. Behind us, towering high above, a spectacular mountain backdrop that pierces the deep cobalt blue yonder.

At this altitude the rarefied air takes its toll on us mere humans, a light head and dizziness the reward and consequence of too much exertion and too little oxygen. At least until we got used to it, we had to take things steady. In contrast, the Tdi equipped Discoverys seem totally unaffected, well largely anyway.

Several vehicles have suffered over-pressurised and ruptured headertanks. We take an enforced stop when ours blows, jetting green liquid everywhere in a fountain of boiling spray, no steam at this altitude though. The pressure release valve had become clogged by dust and the recent combination of extremes was just too much for it. Mark and Damien execute a running repair using Loctite and gaffer tape. Hopefully this will suffice until a proper weld can be completed by the Land Rover boys.

Created by melting snow thousands of feet up in the Andes, a small cascade of crystal clear, ice cool water provides an ideal supply of mineral rich refreshment. It'll still need a 'Puritab', seems a shame really, but better safe than sorry.

Another rather more expected problem is punctures and during one of our regrouping halts Mark lends a little muscle to the perpetual task of repair.

CAMEL
HASTA LA VISTA BABY

Eventually the terrain reaches a plateau, a vast arid semi-desert wasteland. So harsh is the ground that the next few kilometres have to be driven at a snail's pace. Too much velocity here and we could easily do serious damage, even to our ultra strong and resilient Land Rovers.

CAMEL
TROPHY

Inside the UK team Discovery there's a place for everything. With dust masks on, we make our way cautiously across the unforgiving terrain.

Etienne van Eeden carefully pilots the SA Disco. He pays particular attention to select a route avoiding large rocks, those capable of hitting and damaging a vulnerable diff case.

From our position at the rear of the convoy we in the UK Discovery are offered a superb view of the long train of Land Rovers as it snakes through the high sierras of the eastern Andes. Our target is Payogasta, and we must get there tonight no matter what. Only then will Camel Trophy halt for two days whilst the Andean Research Facility is constructed for donation to the local University of Salta.

DEFENDER
CAMEL
TROPHY

Doc Mike Irani in the medical support 110 Defender leads a rather more sleek Discovery as they gingerly meander across the scrub and rock littered terrain.

High up in the Andes this old lady appeared as if from nowhere, trekking across the harsh and inhospitable wilderness, destination unknown. Her time tarnished features tell their own story.

Carlos Martinez and Jorge Corella prepare to follow the medic 110 down into a deep dry river washout.

CAMEL
TROPHY
L430 VAC

CAMEL
TROPHY

The opposite side is even steeper requiring lots of power and inertia to climb successfully as Damien Taft discovers in the UK vehicle, retreating for a second attempt. The sun is going down but we still have many more kilometres to cover before reaching Payogasta, and it's 04:20 before we finally get there. It had been a long day and an even longer night.

At Payogasta some of the kids were keen to make a mark on Camel Trophy in their own personal way.

Graduating mountains that stretch for many miles into the distance provide a majestic backdrop to our campsite. The two day sojourn here provides a welcome opportunity to restock and repair, both physically and mentally, before undertaking our long and demanding crossing of the Andes, the high point of Camel Trophy '94.

In order to construct the Andean Research Centre in the allotted time span, work needs to be carried out around the clock. For this purpose the teams are split into two groups, each working six hours on, six hours off for four periods. The building was complete by noon on the second day (27th) permitting time in the afternoon to construct a purpose built access bridge.

Work is completed on schedule and so now we can look forward to rather more relaxed entertainment in the form of the mid-event barbeque. Late in the evening teams are called upon to entertain their fellow adventurers, a feat performed to spectacular effect by Martial Mathieu, a '93 eventer from Switzerland.

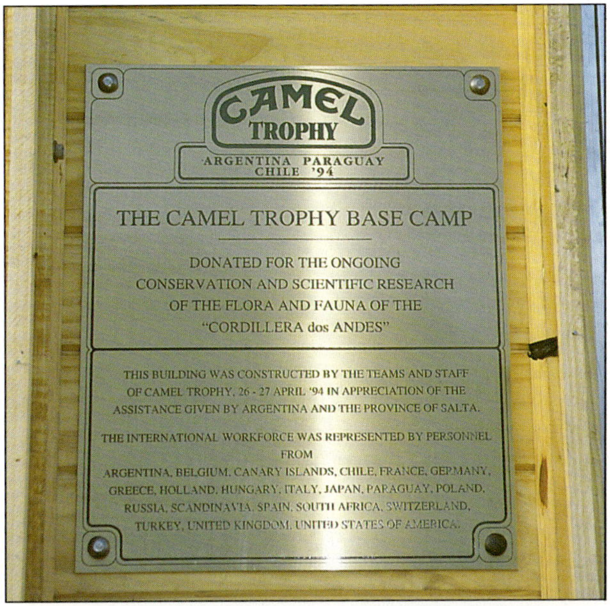

Thursday 28th April Day 13
Bright and early we bid our farewells to Payogasta. Our tasks are complete, our promises kept and it's time for Camel Trophy to venture onwards once again. There's an air of anticipation and of excitement throughout the entire convoy for today we'll be ascending high into the Andes. Before long our 33 strong convoy is separated into small groups, weaving for many kilometres around acute bends and switchbacks, all the time climbing up, up and up. Above and below lies some of the most magnificent and dramatic scenery imaginable, but everything is dwarfed by the snow-tipped mountains that tower thousands of feet over us.

CAMEL
TROPHY
DISCOVERY

Occasionally our ascent is postponed as we encounter a short plateau or ridge. Carine and Jean-Yves lead the South African Discovery as they splash through a shallow stream of chilled melt water.

With great care we follow narrow paths hewn into the rock faces of sheer sided mountains, the tracks winding backwards and forwards as gradually we climb towards our goal. Barely the width of a vehicle there's little room for error. One mistake here, a lapse of concentration and we'd be history, rolling for hundreds perhaps thousands of feet down the side of a mountain.

At 12:00 midday precisely we reach Abra el Acay. At an altitude of 4,985 metres, some 16,000 feet above sea level, this is the highest point on our incredible journey. For many of us it's also the climax of our adventure, affording the most spectacular and emotional views so far. Perhaps we can be forgiven for commemorating this day with an inevitable 'hero' shot. From left to right — the author, Mark Cullum, Damien Taft and 'Chad' Chadderton — alias Team United Kingdom.

Free from pollution and impurities the atmosphere up here is breathtakingly clear, as is the rarefied air which makes one feel a little light headed and dizzy. Consequently rushing around is to be avoided, although this lack of oxygen fails to dissuade fellow Cameleers from indulging in an impromptu, celebratory snowball fight.

With a degree of reluctance we finally depart Abra el Acay to begin a gradual descent. Later we will arrive at San Antonio de los Cobres where we shall rendezvous with the 'Train to the Clouds'. On board is Press Group B and amongst their number Richard Thomas, then editor of the international motoring magazine Land Rover Owner.

CAMEL
TROPHY

A frequently seen member of the indigenous population, this hardy llama's thick fur coat provides ideal protection against dramatically low temperatures and biting wind.

The environment up here is harsh and takes few prisoners. Even creatures specifically equipped for the terrain can succumb to its ferocity.

Our descent towards San Antonio introduces somewhat more substantial roads, permitting a rather more brisk pace.

San Antonio provides an ideal opportunity to once again quench our Discoverys' insatiable appetite for diesel fuel. The drums of JET A-1 are intended for the support helicopter, not the Discos!

The Japanese let fly their rather bent and battered Discovery. The damage had been caused while under tow behind a rigid A-frame. Waka hit a jumbo sized pothole losing control of the vehicle, the Discovery flipping onto its side, very nearly dragging the towing Land Rover workshop vehicle with it. Fortunately what might have been a serious accident resulted in nothing more than bent and bruised panels and egos, together with perhaps a few yen off the vehicle's resale value.

CAMEL
TROPHY
Tadashi Iio

What an incredible place this is, for all the Universe we could be driving on the moon. In keeping with such a notion only the hardiest of plant growth can subsist on this arid and dry land, a lunar landscape that is friend to neither animal nor vegetable.

The convoy dashes across a massive salt flat, similar to the kind used for speed record stuff, although our Discos probably won't be competitive — at least not today.

Team Scandinavia adorn their vehicle with a suitably poignant reminder of the potential hostility of the Andes.

Friday 29th April Day 14
We're en route for Socompa Pass and the border between Argentina and Chile, the third and final country on our incredible journey.

At Socompa Pass, whilst we once again await the slow legal process of passport checking, Boris Kazankin seizes the opportunity to plot our route so far.

Meanwhile the team from Hungary prefer to catch up on lost shuteye.

Even though we're still 3,865 metres above sea level Socompa Pass is dwarfed by the magnificent backdrop of the Andes.

Finally the government is satisfied and we're permitted to depart Socompa and continue our journey. Heading directly into the setting sun, the combination of glare and dust conspires on occasion to make visibility difficult in the extreme. Next stop the Atacama Desert.

Arrive Atacama campsite 01:00 and quickly pitch tents, allowing for direction of wind which is blowing with great force across the plain. Windchill factor takes the ambient temperature way below freezing — a real shock to the system after the past couple of weeks. Saturated in darkness it's impossible at the moment to see anything of our surroundings. Mark fires up the MSR cooker to prepare a slap-up Wayfayrer dinner before retiring to bed.

Camel Campsight Atacama. Daylight of morning arrives, revealing the stark beauty of our surroundings, smack bang in the middle of the Atacama Desert. It's the world's driest too having not received a life sustaining drop of rain since 1926. Gasp!

What a desolate but magnificent place this is. With zero humidity the air is as dry as the sand but also fresh and invigorating. During our two day stop in the Atacama we are scheduled to perform two navigational exercises using GPS (Global Positioning System), the results of which will form part of the final collection of special tasks.

Working in groups we have six hours to use the GPS to locate as many pre-determined waypoints as possible. Supplied coordinates are fed into the GPS handsets and then it's up to the teams to combine the use of these highly accurate instruments with map and compass and complete their search.

Monday 2nd May Day 17
Expanding plumes of fine dust are carried away by the strong morning wind as the convoy departs La Rioja, last night's campsite. Our destination is Tierra del Plata, venue for the final set of special tasks.

As we head towards the final series of special tasks at Tierra del Plata, there's a kind of sadness. We are reaching the end of our dramatic expedition across South America and the culmination of Camel Trophy '94.

However, for Team UK all such thoughts are soon displaced by nervewracking apprehension when, shortly before a night Terratrip exercise in the desert we suffer a jammed transfer box. Working under extreme pressure the Land Rover support crew perform wonders, locating and rectifying the problem with just minutes to spare.

The 'Time Trial Combination' task. Each pair of Cameleers in turn drive up, and then back down this narrow, snaking track. Their runs are timed and need to be as close to each other as possible. Vehicle clocks and personal timepieces are forbidden so alternative, imaginative means of estimating time are employed, methods such as counting wiper sweeps.

Lead Scout Marc Day enjoys the show as the UK duo perform their runs to perfection, no faults and near identical times. The boys are confident of a good result — at least until they're disqualified for being outside the maximum four minute duration. Scrupulous examination and understanding of the rules are an essential prerequisite for these tasks. It's all too easy to mess up on a simple oversight or error.

The next task involves vehicle recovery. A Discovery needs to be winched up a 45° incline and then, using this as anchor, a second and a third follow suit. To permit the first vehicle to be winched up, a sturdy ground anchor has been dug deep into the rocky terrain.

For this exercise the teams had once again been divided into six groups of three, our good friends the South Africans and Russians joining forces with Team UK. Alexandre Davidov feeds the winch cable out to Mark Cullum in preparation for bringing the first vehicle up the steep incline.

Alex's partner Boris Kasankin controls the Discovery's powerful Superwinch from inside the vehicle.

As soon as the Russian vehicle is safely up it can be used as an anchor for the South African and British Discoverys to winch from. Under the supervision of Etienne van Eeden the winch cable has been run back through a snatch block, effectively doubling its potential pulling power.

These three teams worked efficiently together and it seemed only a matter of minutes before the third and last vehicle was on its way up. Damien stands by as Klaus Hass prepares to take tension on the cable.

DEFENDER
CAMEL TROPHY
K318 YKV

The final task of Camel Trophy '94 is performed by all 18 teams simultaneously, albeit subdivided into three groups of six. This task is simply a race to get two support 110 Defenders plus all six national Discoverys across an acute 'V' gulley.

The first thing the teams need to do is platform that acute angle at the bottom of the gulley. Carine and Christel help 'womanhandle' spare XCLs into place. With sand ladders positioned on top, these will successfully perform the job.

As soon as the 110 Defenders are up …

... it's the turn of the team's own Discoverys. Carine, safely ensconced in the cab of Team USA's vehicle, carefully follows her compatriot's instructions as she commands the vehicle's winch.

CAMEL

Wednesday 4th May Day 19
For the last time on Camel Trophy '94 convoy, we have packed our kit away. Next on the agenda is the official 'You Made It' ceremony, in preparation for which our vehicles are once again adorned with national flags. Then each drives into the 'arena' individually, to be greeted by the rapturous applause and cheering of fellow competitors and support crews.

CAMEL
YOU MADE IT

University of Adventure, Class of '94. It's the official end of Camel Trophy 1994 and there stand 36 scruffy and tired but nevertheless happy and fulfilled Cameleers. They've lived out a dream, an experience of a lifetime that each and every one will remember with pride for many years to come.
Next stop Playa de Hornitos, venue for the final banquet and award ceremony. The evening proved to be a fitting finale and one that few of us will ever forget, the celebrations raging well into the next morning. However before the serious merriment could begin Camel Trophy had to be awarded. For the first time in the event's history it was presented to Spain, a deserved victory for the highly capable and well liked pairing of Carlos Martinez and Jorge Corella. To the delight of us all the equally prestigious 'Team Spirit' award was presented to the amiable and ever happy South Africans Etienne and Klaus.

There was good news for the team from the United Kingdom too. Second place in both 'Trophy and Spirit' – an excellent and deserving result of which Mark and Damien can be justly proud. They might well smile the morning after. As D & M are keen to exclaim, Good One!!